New Orleans

Text by Jan Arrigo

Photographs by Laura A. McElroy

Voyageur Press

Edited by Margret Aldrich
Designed by Maria Friedrich
Printed in the United States

05   06   07   08   5   4   3   2

Library of Congress Cataloging-in-Publication Data

Arrigo, Jan, 1960—
  New Orleans / text by Jan Arrigo ; photographs by Laura A. McElroy.
        p. cm.
  ISBN 0-89658-547-6 (hardcover)
  1. New Orleans (La.)—Pictorial works. 2. New Orleans
(La.)—Guidebooks. I. McElroy, Laura A., 1951- II. Title. III. Series.
  F379.N543 A77 2002
  917.63'350464—dc21

                                    2002007537

Distributed in Canada by Raincoast Books, 9050 Shaughnessy Street, Vancouver, B.C. V6P 6E5

Published by Voyageur Press, Inc.
123 North Second Street, P.O. Box 338, Stillwater, MN 55082 U.S.A.
651-430-2210, fax 651-430-2211
books@voyageurpress.com
www.voyageurpress.com

Educators, fundraisers, premium and gift buyers, publicists, and marketing managers:
Looking for creative products and new sales ideas? Voyageur Press books are available at special discounts when purchased in quantities, and special editions can be created to your specifications. For details contact the marketing department at 800-888-9653.

Page 1: *The LaBranche Building was built for the widow of a wealthy sugar planter. This Greek Revival–style home is located on Royal Street in the French Quarter.*

Page 4: *A trombone player from a French Quarter jazz parade pauses to hit a low note.*

Page 5: *This 1700s brick-between-post Creole cottage, Lafitte's Blacksmith Shop, may hold the stash of the pirates Jean and Pierre Lafitte's ill-gotten gains, according to local legend.*

Dedication

To my father, the late Joe Arrigo, whose art, books, and music represent the soul of New Orleans.
—Jan Arrigo

To my dear parents, Kathleen and the late Soulé "Boots" McElroy, for teaching me to search my heart to find my dreams, to pursue my dreams with passion balanced by integrity, and to always thank God for placing the dreams in my heart and providing the ways to fulfill them.
—Laura A. McElroy

Acknowledgments

Special thanks to Julie and David Menasco, Josie Occhipinti, Amelia Durand, Rob Schauffler, Melodie Matyas, Monique May, Jim May, the New Orleans Tourist Commission, Carla Gauthier Lorenz, Charles Gremillion, Mark Monte, Mark Lescale, Arthur Hardy, Pete Fountain, Dickie Brennan and Dick Brennan Sr., John Califano, and Bryan Eichhorn.
—Jan Arrigo

I would like to thank the wonderful people of New Orleans and surrounding areas who graciously helped me to capture the heart of this wonderful area. I extend a personal, heartfelt thank you to: The New Orleans Jazz and Heritage Festival, the Shrimp and Petroleum Festival, the Swamp Festival, and the Spring Fiesta for allowing me photographic access to these great celebrations; Mid City Lanes Rock N' Bowl, Beauregard Keyes House, Edgar Degas House, Longue Vue House and Gardens, Blaine Kern's Mardi Gras World, and the Delta Steamboat Company for allowing me to photograph these wonderful sites; Pete Fountain who so graciously allowed me to photograph him on his day off; Lil' Cajun Swamp Tours for teaching me so much about alligators, shrimping, swamps, and Cajun hospitality; Metairie Marriott Courtyard staff for their invaluable assistance; Robert, Candy, Jim, and Vanessa at Moldaner's Photo Imaging for befriending me and the care with which they developed the film that are images in this book; Commander's Palace, the Palace Cafe, Dickie Brennan's Steakhouse, Mr. B's Bistro, Red Fish Grill, and Gallatoire's for inviting me into your restaurants, for the beautiful dishes the chefs prepared for me to photograph, and for the opportunity to sample the mouth-watering food after the photo sessions ended; and my best friends Bob and Georgia Johnson for their help as photographic assistants and their encouragement throughout every stage of this book.
—Laura A. McElroy

Contents

Introduction

Welcome to New Orleans . . . Y'all Are Pretty, Too!

My sister and some friends were enjoying their annual ladies' outing at the famous Commander's Palace restaurant in the Garden District of New Orleans. As they waited at the bar for their table, sipping pre-lunch Cosmos, they noticed an older woman in a red knit suit with matching pumps and a lacquered bob. The woman approached, coolly appraising them, and then her eyes met directly with Leslie's—the blonde head-turner of the group. The matron looked at her and held her hand out, giving a firm, perfumed handshake. "You are a beautiful girl!" she said theatrically in a booming, mint-julep-dripping accent. All chatter stopped and the bar became quiet. "I'm Mrs. Dolmas,"* the matron declared, her syllabication lingering pointedly over the consonants of her surname. Her eyes then scanned the women's dresses, shoes, and handbags. She

pursed her lips and upon being summoned to her table, motioned with a backhanded wave of her fingers, adding as an afterthought, "And y'all are pretty, too."

This name has been changed to protect the actual woman.

Above: *Painted masks are a popular souvenir with visitors. These decorative masks recall the original styles worn at early Carnival society balls.*

Facing page: *Music fills the square in front of St. Louis Cathedral. Entrepreneurial musicians stake their turf early in the day to fill their coffers by night.*

New Orleanians have a keen interest in the way others perceive them. It's a kind of collective narcissism from a people who both defend and embrace a gracious way of life that holds traditions dear, regardless of how odd or seemingly archaic. Take weddings for example. There's a tradition that before the cake is cut, a small group of the bride's closest single friends gather around the base of it, each one standing in front of a corresponding protruding ribbon. After a signal is given, the ribbons are pulled from the cake to reveal individual trinkets. The unlucky girls receive an iron or thimble, symbolizing an unmarried life, while other girls pull anchors or clovers from the cake, symbolizing luck. Of course, the luckiest bachelorette is the one who pulls out the tiny wedding ring, which promises matrimony. In the Big Easy, logic is often anything but, yet somehow it all makes sense to the people who reside in a city that is more than just a blank backdrop for life.

I should know.

I was born in New Orleans and lived in a house off an avenue called Elysian Fields—the very same atmospheric avenue described in Tennessee Williams's *A Streetcar Named Desire*. Elysian Fields, from the Greek "Elysium," refers to a mythological place of perfect peace and happiness. This feels right, because growing up along that avenue was idyllic for me. Just a few blocks away from our house was the Pontchartrain Beach Amusement Park where "You have fun, you have fun, everyday of the week." I knew this advertising slogan to be absolutely true—if only my parents would have agreed. Alas, the amusement park is gone now, but there's still plenty of amusement in this town and happily much of it is free!

Yes, the terrain of mudbugs and mayhem boasts enough to do, see, and eat to last one's lifetime without ever getting bored. New Orleans is a town where:

- Drive-through daiquiri shops coexist with daily Catholic masses.
- Whoever gets the tiny plastic baby that's buried inside a King Cake (a coffeecake pastry that looks like a giant donut) has to buy the next one.
- The Krewe of Crawfish, an informal group of crustacean-loving friends, parades inside Whitey's seafood restaurant. Riders are pushed around on dollies decorated as floats, and the "king" waves to his subjects from a rolling commode.
- The 1960s hit song "Mother-in-Law" is played over and over at the Ernie K-Doe Mother-in-Law Lounge simply because it's the only selection available on the jukebox.
- An impromptu multigenerational line dance forms right in the middle of St. Charles Avenue when "Don't Mess with My Toot Toot" is played on a speaker system the Sunday before Mardi Gras.
- My friend Monique once rode up to a bar—that is, *inside* the bar—and ordered a drink while on the back of a horse named Freckles, and no one said a word.

Welcome to my world.

Where Y'at: Geography as Destiny

Instead of saying "How are you?" in New Orleans we say, "Where y'at?" The literal translation of this slang dialect being "Where are you at?" So where you is, is where you at. Got that?

Where you are in the Crescent City turns out to be more than a matter of semantics. The bend in the Mississippi River deals a kind of directional wild card. Let's say you're in New Orleans approaching the West Bank. Well, you're really going east. Confusing? Next add pea soup fog and a winding river you thought you'd already crossed and you're smack in the middle of a disorienting recipe.

If geography is destiny, then New Orleans, built on swampland that wades below sea level and surrounded by the terra firma of the Bible belt, is destined to be an eccentric outpost of the exotic and the provincial. The city is situated on the banks of the Mississippi on a crescent-shaped piece of land (hence the Crescent City nickname), bordered on the north by Lake Pontchartrain, and crisscrossed with bayous and canals. This watery environment has created some bizarre scenarios—including alligators in drainage canals and floating caskets—and leads one to wonder why such an improbable location was ever selected for a city to be built upon.

N'awlins History 101

It all began with a land scam. John Law, a Scottish real estate financier living in France, scoped out the Louisiana Territory—the area that French explorer René Robert Cavelier, Sieur de La Salle, had claimed and named for the Sun King, Louis XIV—and decided it was ripe for a ruse. He advertised the land with lavish promises of fabulous wealth and was so convincing that in 1717 the crown handed over a twenty-five-year charter for him to scoop up more land. Law then had Jean Baptiste Le Moyne, Sieur de Bienville, establish a new settlement in the Louisiana Territory, and the spot chosen was named after the Duke of Orléans: La Nouvelle Orléans. That's New Orleans in plain English.

Of course, there were people already living here. The Choctaw tribe founded the oldest street in the city, Bayou Road, which follows Bayou St. John to the Mississippi River and was an early trail and portage. They also introduced filé, the powdered, dried leaves of the sassafras tree that is a key ingredient used in gumbos. Many Choctaws intermarried with the new settlers, but tragically most of the tribe eventually killed or forced off their land by encroachers.

The French adventurers encountered the Choctaws were also greeted by swarms of bloodthirsty mosquitoes that managed to find their way inside the explorers' crude huts made from palmetto leaves. The settlers toughed it out, but soon found themselves overtaken by the Spanish, who had obtained the rights to the land in the secret 1762 Treaty of Fontainebleau, which became the official Treaty of Paris in 1763. Meanwhile, in New England, the colonies were revolting against England. A local hero of the revolution, Oliver Pollock (who donated capital for ammunition and supplies) helped New Orleans side with Spain, whose flag would continue to wave over the Crescent City through fires, population expansion, and a flourishing seaport. All was fine until a certain diminutive French general with a distinctive comb-over came to town.

In 1800, Napoleon Bonaparte talked Spain into giving the Louisiana Territory back to France with the Treaty of San Ildefonso. U.S. President Thomas Jefferson pressured Napoleon, however, and in 1803 the beleaguered general gave in and sold New Orleans and the entire Louisiana Territory to the United States for $15 million. Although he never actually slept in the building built for him, the atmospheric Napoleon House, now a bar and grill, is a great place to order a Pimm's Cup cocktail and contemplate Napoleon's still-strong influence on New Orleans. For example, Louisiana is the only state that uses the Roman-based Napoleonic code of law. If all this history makes you curious about what he actually looked like, you can study his death mask, which is on view at the Cabildo. The site of the signing of the Louisiana Purchase, the Cabildo on Jackson Square is now a museum with a fascinating historical collection.

Another early group of New Orleanians—the one that actually built the city—was made up of West African slaves, many of who came from that continent via the Caribbean. They cleared the swampland that is now the French Quarter, or Vieux Carré (Old Square), and dug the canals and streets. Forbidden to express themselves through writing or speech, they found a collective voice through music, song, and dance at Congo Square. By 1840, New Orleans had the largest population of free people of color in the United States, and Congo Square became an outdoor market and cultural haven for all people of color.

The original heart of New Orleans's Central Business District (CBD), Carondelet Street, features classic bank buildings made of limestone.

They Liked It Here So Much, They Stayed

The New Orleans board of education requires every eighth-grade student to study the history of their city and state. Here's a peek at a timeline study sheet of the inhabitants of New Orleans:

Before anybody: alligators and mosquitoes!

Native Americans: Choctaw, Chickasaw, Natchez, Opelousa, and other tribes.

1534: Spaniard Hernando de Soto visits the Gulf South after hearing about the area from countryman Alvar Nunez Cabeza de Vaca.

1682: Frenchman René Robert Cavelier, Sieur de La Salle, proclaims the broad area around the Mississippi River Louisianne for Louis XIV.

1698: French-Canadian Pierre Le Moyne, Sieur d'Iberville, checks out the area and founds the settlement of Louisiana.

1718: French-Canadian Jean Baptiste Le Moyne, Sieur de Bienville (Pierre's brother), establishes New Orleans and populates the city with French convicts.

1720s: Lured by Scotsman John Law's hyperbolic handbills, German peasants settle on the West Bank, and the area is named Cote des Allemands.

1720s: Slaves from West Africa and West India arrive.

1766–1803: New Orleans's first Spanish governor, Don Antonio de Ulloa, rules and brings a delegation of his countrymen with him.

1755: French-speaking Acadians (corrupted as "Cajun") are expelled from Nova Scotia by the British and settle along the banks of the Mississippi River above New Orleans.

1791–1804: A wave of free people of color comes in from Haiti.

1830s: Irish settlers arrive, fleeing the potato famine in their country.

1890s: Sicilians begin arriving, escaping the agricultural and social hardships of their country. Most settle in or near the French Quarter, which was then called "Little Italy."

1960s: Cubans come to New Orleans after Fidel Castro takes over the island of Cuba.

1970s: Vietnamese arrive following the fall of Saigon. They settle mostly in New Orleans East.

William Faulkner wrote his first novel, Soldiers' Pay, in this house at 624 Pirate's Alley. Open daily, the site offers tours and a bookshop.

The Soul of the City Is Music

Today Congo Square is part of Louis Armstrong Park, named for jazz musician Louis "Satchmo" Armstrong. The park is also the home of WWOZ 90.7 FM, the local radio station that plays all New Orleans music. The neighborhood beyond Congo Square, known as Storyville, was a red light district until the 1930s. It was equally famous for its commerce (prostitution) and its music (Louis Armstrong was born there).

What exactly is New Orleans music? It's a complex, musical gumbo with influences of Dixieland jazz, rhythm and blues, gospel, Cajun, Zydeco, and contemporary rock. If you're in town for the springtime New Orleans Jazz and Heritage Festival (a misnomer since the music includes all of the above styles and more) you can hear a variety of sounds on the many stages that are set up inside the Fair Grounds—sans horses! Food and crafts that are indigenous to Louisiana are sold as part of the celebration. If you're lucky enough to be in town for the French Quarter Festival in late April, you can see many local acts like Charlene Neville and Big Al Carson for free.

And if you're in town when there is no music festival, you can always head out to Bourbon Street—which, incidentally, is named for a French duke, not the Kentucky spirit—where there are a number of clubs to explore. The best street for live music, however, is Frenchmen Street, off Esplanade Avenue. Clubs like Café Brasil showcase local talent and attract acts from all over the world. Uptown there's the legendary Tipitina's (Dr. John, The Radiators, and The Nevilles all got started here and call this home base when in town), The Maple Leaf (attracts great Cajun bands), and the very casual River Shack on River Road. Perhaps the most unusual place to hear music and dance is the same place where you can bowl and have a bite. The Mid City Lanes Rock 'N Bowl on Carrollton Avenue is large and loud and can get very crowded when a big-name Cajun band appears, but the raucous atmosphere of toppled pins, ceiling fans, and 1950s décor can't be beat. And no, you don't have to rent shoes if you're not bowling!

Happily there are music clubs and bars in most neighborhoods, due to the fact that there were no ordinance codes until the 1930s. That's probably because the city grew from a collective of disconnected suburbs,

Legendary Dixieland clarinetist Pete Fountain, the man who once broke Lawrence Welk's bubble machine, now plays in his own Hilton Hotel club.

called *faubourgs*, as opposed to most cities where the opposite is true. These neighborhoods have a range of house styles including Creole cottages, shotgun houses, and porched-in bungalows, which were built off the ground because the city lies below sea level. Before the levees were built, an especially heavy rainstorm meant that a raised house would afford a dry walk to the bedroom versus a soggy one.

Peeling Back a City's Psyche

The constant threat of total inundation from one last ferocious hurricane (or just a particularly brutal thunderstorm) results in a fatalistic attitude held together with a combination of firewater and holy water. Weather forecasters have been known to say that if the right circumstances occurred in wind velocity and rain, the city would be a sitting punchbowl filled with the murky waters of the Mississippi and Lake Pontchartrain overflowing into the streets. Yet some devil-may-care types still have hurricane parties!

Incongruous New Orleans—where anything can happen—often combines the surreal and the traditional. For example, Voodoo and the Catholic Church happily coexist here. So do the gay Southern Decadence Festival and the religious blessing of the fleet at the Shrimp and Petroleum Festival—itself an especially curious combination! These dichotomies are a constant theme that transcends geography and goes right to the very soul of the city's personality. The dualities result in a push-pull effect: the "push" of the Big Easy being the weather, with its unpredictable winters and sultry summers, and the "pull" being its food, music, and people, as well as the sensual nature of the city. For example, in New Orleans you can:

- Watch the dramatic, swirling river currents of the Mississippi while sipping champagne at the Bella Luna restaurant.
- Hear Lady B. J. sing while you're sitting snug at Snug Harbor on Frenchman Street.
- Inhale the natural perfume of the oleander bush while walking through the Garden District.
- Take a River Road drive and stop at Destrehan Plantation for a tour through history.
- Feel Spanish moss for the first time and discover its springy, ropelike texture, while you imagine ancestors stuffing furniture with it.
- Catch heads of cabbage thrown like volleyballs off floats at St. Patrick's Day parades.
- Take in the heady aroma of café au lait and beignets.
- Slurp turtle soup with a shot of sherry at Mandina's on Canal Street.

Food is an important element in everyday New Orleans life, and it also plays a key role in festival rituals. St. Joseph's Day, for example, is an important local religious

Louis Armstrong Park, which honors the jazz great, is part of New Orleans Jazz Park. The area incorporates Congo Square, an important early jazz site.

celebration that has its roots in historic Sicily, where the saint was credited with ending a drought. In thanksgiving, food offerings were made. Sicilians who came to New Orleans brought this tradition with them. They prepare an altar of food that includes a cookie called *cuccidata*, which is sculpted into wreaths, hearts, crosses, and even the staff and beard of St. Joseph himself. These altars are set up in people's homes and church centers for viewing. A delicious, hot pasta meal is then served and donations accepted. People rarely leave empty handed. Cookies or biscotti flavored with almond, anise, vanilla, and other spices are given away, but probably the most popular gift is the "Lucky Bean." Fava beans are dried and blessed as a remembrance of St. Joseph and are to be kept in one's possession as a blessing for protection—or *portafortuna* as they say in Sicily.

Y'all Tawk Funny

They never seem to get it right in the movies—the New Orleans accent, that is. Either it's too Cajun, like Dennis Quaid in *The Big Easy,* or too saccharin and southern drawly. But the truth is, if you ask a native New Orleanian about his accent, you will most likely get a blank stare. That's because most believe they speak without any accent at all! So what do we really sound like? Think "N'Awlins" or "N'yawlyns" but never "Noo Orleens." Or, better yet, just listen to Harry Connick Jr. or television chef Emeril Lagasse speak. That's it!

Hey, Suitcase! The Importance of Nicknames in New Orleans

They were all lined up side by side in folding aluminum chairs facing Veteran's Highway, waiting for the Irish/Italian parade to begin. First was Maw Maw, my ninety-three-year-old grandmother, sitting shaded under a large black parasol. Next was her daughter, my Aunt Mary, then Uncle Tony, who sat with my parents. My brother, his wife, and my niece stood in the street talking to my two sisters who were sitting on an ice chest filled with beer. The parade commenced, and flying cabbage, carrots, and trinkets thrown from passing floats immediately inundated us. Luckily Maw Maw was kept safe from the flying produce by her umbrella, which now doubled as a protective shield. Next approached rows of marching men wearing pompom-topped berets and holding Styrofoam canes packed with green-dyed carnations, which they plucked out one at a time to give to special ladies in exchange for kisses. I ducked into the crowd when a red-faced, bulbous-nosed octogenarian approached me with a carnation and a meaningful look. Meanwhile, behind the marching men came a car of lo-

This Audubon Zoo alligator suns himself in surroundings built to resemble his habitat in the Louisiana swampland.

cal Italian-American dignitaries sitting on the back seat ledge of a convertible, waving casually. Suddenly my brother shouted, "Hey, Suitcase! Suitcase!" But the men were too busy smiling and tossing doubloons to hear. My brother turned to Uncle Tony, "Wasn't that Suitcase?" Turns out that Suitcase got his nickname from a problem marriage, which had him packing on a frequent basis.

Yes, nicknames are big here. There was a sportscaster named Hap that lived in "Chilly Gentilly," the suburb spanning Elysian Fields that goes out to Lake Pontchartrain. I had an aunt named Nootsie, and my mother is called Butsy. I went to grammar school with an Ernie we called Oyster. My friend Mark has an Aunt Shrimp, and there's a Puddin' from New Orleans East. Local politicians have included a Chep, a Dutch, and a Moon. Even the *Times-Picayune* obituaries always include the unique moniker of the deceased in solemn quotes.

Doing Death Rite:
Cities of the Dead

The yellow fever epidemics of the 1800s fostered the New Orleans philosophy of living in the present moment. After all, no one knew where the disease came from or who would be next! It's hard to imagine, but entire families could disappear in one summer, and funerals to bury a multitude of dead bodies were a daily reality for those who survived. But there was a technical problem with all of those burials in a city that lies below sea level.

After a rainstorm, the coffins would float.

While boring holes into the coffin bottoms so water could enter and force the coffin to sink quickly solved that problem, the final solution was to build tombs above ground. And so, New Orleans honors its deceased in cemeteries that are more like cities of the dead. Many of the tombs feature magnificent funerary sculpture with artistic styles ranging from Egyptian to Roman to Beaux-Arts. A walk among these tombs makes one feel a kind of hopeful peace for both the past and one's own final ending. Daily tours are available in many of these cemeteries. Some of the most historic and interesting ones include:

- St. Louis Cemetery No. 1 (1789), Basin Street between St. Louis and Conti Streets
- St. Louis Cemetery No. 3 (1856), 3421 Esplanade Avenue
- City of Lafayette Cemetery No. 1 (1833), Washington Avenue between Prytania and Sixth Streets
- St. Roch's Cemeteries No. 1 and No. 2 (1874), 1725 St. Roch Avenue

The ritual of bringing flowers to cemeteries and sprucing up tombs is a New Orleans tradition on All Saints Day, which falls on November 1.

Now enjoy Laura McElroy's beautiful photography, which captures the essence of life in New Orleans. Explore the amazing architecture, music, food, and people that shape the Big Easy's distinct personality. When you are finished and place this book on your coffee table, we hope you will return to its pages again and again, as it lures you back to this fascinating city.

If not, well . . . y'all are pretty, too.

The Big Easy Spirit

Slow. Easy. Big. These three words aptly describe New Orleans. Residents cook gumbo and red beans and rice slow and easy. Simmer, then serve. They walk down the street slow and easy, taking their time to smile at strangers or say hello to neighbors in a drawn-out, studied drawl. People approach life here with an intuitive ease that can often be misinterpreted. Lazy? Sometimes. But it's hot here, and energy must be reserved for important things like fun, food, and enjoying life.

Now there are lots of things big here—dinner portions (like the seafood platter); wide "neutral grounds" (the street medians); oak trees (whose extending branches are hefty enough for kids to ride); and girth (big bellies abound)—but the biggest commodity here is heart. In fact, if you are being served a meal, or having your shoes shined or your hair cut, it's quite possible that you will be addressed as "heart" (pronounced "hawt"). As in, "Ya want that sandwich dressed, hawt?" Or, "More iced tea, hawt?"

Yep, it's a friendly bunch. A few years ago some friends and I were wearily walking out of the Jazz and Heritage Festival grounds, slowly making our way back to the car, when a young, multi-pigtailed little girl waved us over with a plate of crawfish. She invited us to join her family on their front lawn, where they had set up a newspaper-covered card table with freshly boiled crustaceans and cold Dixie beer. Now that's hospitality.

The spirit of the Big Easy lies within the very visible soul of its inhabitants. So pay attention, hawt, you may learn something from the people and neighborhoods that are truly the heart of this city.

Above: *A breathtaking sunrise on the Mississippi River. The origin of the waterway's name comes from the Algonquin Indians, in whose language* misi *means "great" and* sipi *means "water."*

Facing page: *This Mardi Gras masker enjoys relative anonymity, as his ornately plumed headdress obscures his features.*

The John James Audubon boat tour offers excellent city views along its seven-mile cruise between the Aquarium of the Americas and the Audubon Zoo.

Top right: *This classic Natchez steamer departs daily from the Jax Brewery dock for a fascinating tour up the Mississippi River.*

Bottom right: *Harry Hypolite, playing with Nathan and the Zydeco Cha Chas, serves up his unique guitar rhythms at the New Orleans Jazz and Heritage Festival.*

Facing page: *Mr. B., an elder statesman of carriage tour guides, smiles with his mule in front of Jackson Square.*

Top: *Lively second-liners demonstrate the tradition of breaking into an informal processional dance to celebrate the lives of the deceased at this mock jazz funeral.*

Bottom left: *Boiled shrimp is prepared with a variety of seasonings, which are added to the boiling water so the flavor is effused within the shrimp, potatoes, and corn.*

A master shucker serves the delicious treat of raw oysters at Felix's, a popular Bourbon Street restaurant.

Top left: *Hidden gems, the courtyards found in the French Quarter were the coolest "rooms" available before air conditioning.*

Bottom left: *These stylish, wide-brimmed hats offer a smart solution to the year-round, bright New Orleans sunlight.*

Lush ferns line the balcony of the Pontalba Apartments. The landmark Jackson Square buildings were home to author Sherwood Anderson in 1922.

Facing page: *Dating back to 1750, Ursuline Convent is the only French Colonial–style building to survive two major fires that swept the city in the 1700s.*

Above: *The Jesuit Gothic Revival–style Most Holy Name of Jesus Church was built next to Loyola University in 1914.*

Above and right: *Balconies offer an outdoor room with a view. These private areas double as comfortable viewing platforms to the street life below.*

Facing page: *Gibson Hall, Tulane University's Romanesque Revival stone building, faces St. Charles Avenue, with Loyola University next door.*

Facing page: *This historic Esplanade Avenue home, which features gingerbread trim and stained-glass windows, is a striking example of ornate New Orleans architecture.*

Above: *The Crescent City Market, located at Magazine and Girod Streets, sells flowers, food, and more and is open on Saturdays from 8 A.M. to noon.*

Left: *Known as the Thirteen Sisters, this intact row of 1833 Anglo-American, Federal-style townhouses on Julia Street now offers art and craft galleries, as well as apartments and studios.*

This historic home near Bayou St. John features a lush sago palm in the foreground.

The Pitot House Museum, an eighteenth-century West Indies plantation home located on Bayou St. John, offers a sublime view of its balcony.

Resembling a Dutch landscape painting, this Bayou St. John photo depicts grassy embankments created by the Works Progress Administration (WPA) in the 1930s. Today, this area is a great place to bike, stroll, or canoe.

Facing page: *Boardwalk views from the winding paths of Jean Lafitte National Historical Park in the Barataria Preserve feature up-close glimpses of wetland life, such as these wild purple irises.*

Above: *Captain Cyrus Blanchard, of Lil' Cajun Swamp Tours leads two-hour cruises through Bayou Barataria. Tours include a visit with Julie, his pet alligator.*

Left: *The magnolia was chosen as the state flower in 1900 but was once challenged by members of the Louisiana Iris Society.*

Overleaf: *Cyprus trees stand in Slidell's Honey Island Swamp, northeast of New Orleans across Lake Pontchartrain. Dr. Paul Wagner's swamp tours are guided by knowledgeable biologists.*

Let the Good Times Roll

One morning I stopped in a New Orleans drugstore with some out-of-town pals to buy some liquor. That's right, drugstores sell booze here. Somewhat more bizarre though, all of the spirits are kept locked up in a cabinet behind the counter, requiring a key. As I approached the counter, I noticed an elderly clerk surreptitiously eating a hard-boiled egg in the corner. After gingerly popping the yoke in her mouth, she shuffled over to me in her white nurse's dress, stopped, and pulled her purple hairnet forward. When I requested a fifth of vodka, she looked at me wordlessly and tapped a bell twice with a surprisingly agile, arthritic-looking index finger. She then adjusted a microphone, leaned into it, simultaneously letting out a loud sigh that carried throughout the store, and announced in a slow drawl, "Customa needs liqua." Mortified, I felt the silent annoyance from the sundry-buying—and teetotaling—customers. Then I turned to my friends, smiled, and exclaimed, *"Laissez les bons temps rouler!"* (Let the good times roll!)

The good times roll night and day in New Orleans, as there are no closing laws here. For example, in twenty-four hours you can eat beignets for breakfast; ride a riverboat; have a hot, cheap lunch at Mena's; gamble at Harrah's Casino, then spend your winnings in the shops at Canal Place; chase a goat at the zoo; visit a plethora of museums; have a Pimm's Cup and a mufaletta at Napoleon House; hear live music on Frenchmen Street; and toast the evening's end with a Hurricane at Pat O'Brien's. Hungry again? There's always the Hummingbird Grill where your fellow 4 A.M. diners might include a stripper, a student, or your neighbor that just got out of jail on bail.

A votre santé! (To your health!)

Above: *You can rock (and of course roll) or bowl while you listen to local bands at the popular Mid City Lanes Rock 'N Bowl.*

Facing page: *The sun sets over Lake Pontchartrain, revealing in shadow the world's longest causeway, which leads to the quieter North Shore.*

Facing page: *This mule leads visitors up Royal Street, a popular area for art galleries, shops, and antique stores.*

Above: *Carriage views transport the imagination back in time as buggies wind through the French Quarter.*

Left: *Paddlewheelers, like the American Queen pictured here, were once a way of life along the Mississippi.*

Left: *The New Orleans Museum of Art's newest addition is the five-acre sculpture garden featuring work by Henry Moore, Jacques Lipchitz, and more.*

Above: *The Botanical Garden, located in City Park, features formal flower gardens of over two thousand plant species, both exotic and native to the Gulf South.*

Left: *Blaine Kern's Mardi Gras World, located in the West Bank neighborhood of Algiers Point, lets you see gorgeous floats up close—without the bead-catching distractions of a passing parade!*

Above: *A "flying horse" profile shows one of fifty-four carved wooden animals on the restored antique merry-go-round in City Park's William A. Hines Carousel Gardens.*

Above: *Musicians at the Maison Bourbon (House of Bourbon) serve up sanctified sounds of the city to an audience of believers.*

Right: *Preservation Hall, located at 726 St. Peter Street, offers traditional jazz concerts in thirty-minute sets. The alcohol-free setting is appropriate for the entire family.*

Facing page: *A crimson-clad singer belts out an impromptu ballad, serenading an entire Royal Street block on a sunny afternoon.*

Above: *Bourbon Street clubs, like the Storyville District's Jazz Alley, offer a variety of jazz styles—including Dixieland—on a nightly basis.*

Right: *Bourbon Street is a hotbed of all-night clubs, bars, and restaurants. They will all provide the essential "go-cup," which allows nomadic types to continue drinking on the streets.*

Facing page: *A pink-plumed psychic awaits her next customer (and thus her own fortune) in Jackson Square.*

Above: *For these revelers, pre-Halloween merriment starts with a hearty meal consumed in full costume. (Hey, ya gotta eat!)*

Left: *Gaining a unique perspective of Decatur Street, this boldly balanced unicycler reveals the everyday antics of Jackson Square.*

Facing page: *Street performers like this derby-tipping juggler are a "tip if you like me" attraction to the French Quarter.*

Above: *An angelic human statue stands below the magnificent wrought-iron balconies of Chartres Street.*

The Cuisine Scene: Food as Religion

Food is its own focus in this town of diverse palates and people, but most agree on one thing: It all tastes good! In New Orleans, it's possible to feast on Creole, Cajun, and just about any other kind of cuisine at an impressive selection of restaurants where locals dine next to visitors—always a good sign. Happily, an awesome meal can be had in even the cheapest dive, where a cold pitcher of beer replaces a carafe of Chardonnay and a practical roll of paper towels on the table replaces a cloth napkin in your lap.

If it's Monday, you should order red beans and rice. This first-day-of-the-workweek tradition coincided with laundry day, when a pot of beans could simmer for hours while the wash got done. Kidney beans are slow cooked with any combination of ham hocks, sausage, or pickled pork, and the spicy bean juices are wiped up with crusty French bread. This dish is considered Creole rather than Cajun.

What's the difference? Creole refers to a mixture of West Indian and European (including Spanish) influences. Haute Creole dishes include oysters Bienville and oysters Rockefeller. Cajun is a nickname for Acadians, the French settlers who came to Louisiana by way of Nova Scotia. Cajun country lies to the west of the city, but its spicy cuisine is plentiful in New Orleans. Some great examples of Cajun food include crawfish bisque, crawfish étouffée, and andouille (sausage) gumbo. Both cuisines may include seasonings of cayenne pepper, bay leaves, Tabasco, and Creole mustard. The best cooks all use the "Holy Trinity"—a mixture of white onion, sweet green bell pepper, and celery used to flavor everything from gumbos to meat loaf!

New Orleans cuisine is an experience that should not be missed. If you don't happen to live here, there is an amazing array of cookbooks available on the subject—although nothing compares to eating the real thing. *Bon appetit!*

Above: *Mouth-watering examples of a chilled seafood platter, French bread, and ice-cold draft beer await hungry diners.*

Facing page: *A bustling atmosphere radiates from the Red Fish Grill, a popular seafood restaurant operated by the celebrated Brennan family, who have owned local restaurants for many years.*

Above: *The first catch yields bushels of fresh Bayou Barataria shrimp. Large trawling nets gather the shrimp from the water, which are then sold nationwide.*

Right: *Fresh alligator and turtle meat are among the many unusual choices at the French Market, open daily.*

At Johnny's Po Boys, located at 511 St. Louis Street, hero sandwiches tempt hungry palates. If you want yours with all the trimmings, order it "dressed."

Hot sauces abound at the French Market, where the selection can be daunting. Some Tabasco-sauce peppers come directly from nearby Avery Island.

The po' boy (also known as the "poorboy") dates back to Depression times when a cheap sandwich might be the day's main meal.

These blue crabs, caught in local waters, are especially tasty. Crabs are sold boiled—and sometimes live—in local groceries when in season.

Tangy Crescent City Market Creole tomatoes, often oversized like these voluptuous beauties, make a tasty salad with fresh basil.

Tasty regionally made tomato sauces and jams await eager buyers at the Crescent City Market.

Above: *An employee replenishes the daily stock of fresh fruit and other wares at the Farmer's Market. Pecans (pronounced locally as "pa cohhns," not "pea cans") sold at markets like this one provide a tasty foundation for pies and pralines.*

Facing page: *A quintessential Lucky Dog vendor, one of many located throughout the French Quarter, poses next to his cart. Order your "dog of luck" with a variety of fixings.*

Above: *Early nineteenth-century cooking methods are demonstrated in the still-functioning 1830s Hermann-Grima House kitchen.*

Top right: *A favorite breakfast of café au lait and powdered sugar donuts (called beignets) is served at Café Du Monde, New Orleans's oldest outdoor French Market coffee stand.*

Bottom right: *Café society thrives twenty-four hours a day at the busy Café Du Monde, located across the street from Jackson Square.*

Facing page: *This vendor's produce stand is a Carrollton Avenue landmark.*

Facing page: *Contrasting colors of red and green show historic French doors and a stucco-covered façade. This entryway invites diners into the Déjà vu Grill.*

Above: *Luigi's, the former Progress Grocery on Decatur Street, offers Italian specialties, including fresh muffalettas—olive-salad-based sandwiches stuffed with cold cuts in a circular sesame seed loaf.*

Left: *If it's Monday, you can be sure any restaurant in town will be serving red beans and rice, a time-honored local tradition.*

Overleaf *The famous dish oysters Rockefeller was created at Antoine's in 1899. In continuous operation since 1825, Antoine's first meals were served by the current owner's great grandfather.*

Above: *Here, Executive Chef Michelle McRaney of Mr. B's Bistro prepares barbecued shrimp, which actually aren't barbecued at all—they're sautéed with butter and Worcestershire sauce.*

Top right: *Palace Café pastry chef Toby Dotson displays an incredible selection of delicious desserts. The restaurant is located in a refurbished piano store on Canal Street.*

Bottom right: *Galatoire's, the Friday-afternoon hot spot for lunch, has attracted the "who's who" of the city for decades.*

Delicacies from the menu at Commander's Palace restaurant, located in the heart of the Garden District, include both traditional and modern fare.

A hometown favorite, Felix's serves up fresh oysters. Local legend says to eat raw oysters only in months containing the letter r.

An art-deco neon sign calls to the hungry by listing some favorite dishes. Many restaurants are open twenty-four hours a day.

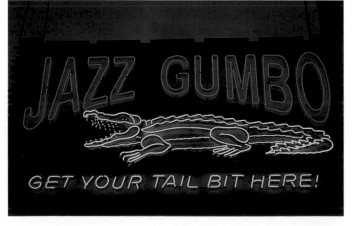

This neon sign incorporates an alligator into its motif—the unofficial mascot of the city.

Oyster shucking can be a full-time profession. This shucker liberates tasty bivalves at the Acme Oyster House.

A Living History City: The Preservation of Architecture and Customs

History can't forget New Orleans for one overwhelming reason: its architecture. They left their mark, the people that came before, with shotgun houses, grilled ironwork, elaborate ceiling medallions, French doors, double-parlors, cemetery monuments that rival museum sculpture, West Indies–style plantations, and Creole cottages.

Today, historic buildings are alive and well—or at least alive and ailing. The sight of a decaying building conjures up romantic thoughts of lives lived and left and creates an opportunity to restore or make new. Renovation is a religion here, and the people who save the city's unique structures are heroes who inspire others to do the same. Before you know it, a whole community can be revitalized and preserved. Julia Street, in the Warehouse District, is a perfect example. Once a skid row, the city's second-oldest neighborhood is now a showplace of living history and home of the Preservation Resource Center.

The French Quarter, or Vieux Carré, is the oldest neighborhood in New Orleans. The uniform grid of the area's 120 square blocks was surveyed in 1722 and once comprised the entire city. Most of the oldest buildings preserved in the French Quarter today, which feature beautiful "iron lace" balconies, are, in fact, Spanish and were built after the fires of 1788 and 1794. In the years just before World War I, however, the area slipped in reputation and became a dangerous slum. Concerned citizens voiced their alarm, and in 1936, the Vieux Carré Commission was formed. Today, many people understand that in preserving New Orleans's structures, the city's customs, rituals, and traditions of its multicultured heritage are kept alive and continue to thrive.

Above: *Christian symbols of angels and crosses adorn the tops of these aboveground tombs located at St. Louis Cemetery No. 3.*

Facing page: *This 1896 Georgian Revival–style home on St. Charles Avenue has been dubbed "The Wedding Cake House" for its fanciful architectural details.*

Top left: *Christmas Eve midnight mass, followed by coffee and donuts at Café du Monde, is a popular ritual with many local Catholics.*

Bottom left: *The patroness of New Orleans and Louisiana, Our Lady of Prompt Succor, looks over the interior of St. Louis Cathedral.*

Above: *The neoclassical décor featured inside the St. Louis Cathedral includes an 1852 Belgium baroque altar screen and a hand-painted ceiling mural.*

Facing page: *Completed in 1851, the St. Louis Cathedral is the centerpiece of Jackson Square. The Good Friday fire of 1788 destroyed an earlier church that had been built on these grounds in 1724.*

Overleaf: *Perfectly symmetrical hanging plants grace the filigreed "iron lace" balcony of the landmark LaBranche Building on Royal Street.*

Left and top image: *Examples of traditional shotgun-style houses are pictured here. The name is derived from the theory that a bullet could be shot straight through the house from front door to back without hitting anything, due to the flow-through style floor plan.*

Bottom image: *This French Quarter home features traditional shuttered doors with movable slats for airflow control.*

Facing page: *The Garden District, located upriver from the French Quarter, is listed on the National Register of Historic Places. Take the St. Charles Avenue streetcar to explore its stately architecture, lush landscaping, and magnolia trees.*

Top left: *The Cornstalk Hotel is an 1890's Queen Anne–style townhouse and a French Quarter landmark treasured for its intricate cast-iron cornstalk fence.*

Bottom left: *This intricate cornstalk fence was created in a Philadelphia foundry for an Antebellum Italianate–style Garden District villa.*

Top left: *How did the Upper middle class live in the mid 1800s? The 1850 Town House Museum reveals Rococo Revival grandeur within.*

Top right: *The spiral staircase is a highlight of Longue Vue House's interior. Tours of the Bamboo Road mansion include walks through eight acres of theme gardens.*

Right: *The 1852 home where French Impressionist painter Edgar Degas once lived is now a bed-and-breakfast, offering historic tours. Featured here is the "Estelle" guestroom.*

Facing page: *A gated entrance leads to the Beauregard-Keyes House, built in 1826. The Chartres Street home opens for tours Monday through Saturday.*

Facing page: *A Metairie Cemetery tomb row is graced with stone-carved Christian motifs. Aboveground tombs are a necessity in a city that lies below sea level.*

Above: *Decorative iron signage welcomes visitors to St. Roch's Cemetery No. 2 and chapel, which was built in 1895.*

Left: *Restoration, such as this stained glass repair work at Metairie Cemetery, is a continual reality within New Orleans's historic cemeteries.*

A statue of New Orleans founder Jean Baptiste Le Moyne, Sieur de Bienville, peers down Decatur Street as if to survey the city he built.

Young scouts contemplate their country's history at the D-Day Museum. The Warehouse District museum features artifacts and information on World War II.

Left: *The St. Charles Avenue streetcar passes Gallier Hall, a mid-nineteenth-century Greek Revival building, which was named for its architect, James Gallier Sr. In 1853, it became the city hall and is now used for civic receptions.*

Above: *Built by the Spanish in 1795–99, the Cabildo is now a museum where visitors can see the room in which the Louisiana Purchase was signed, view Napoleon Bonaparte's death mask, and learn about the history of African Americans in New Orleans.*

Overleaf: *Stately live oaks lead to Oak Alley Plantation built between 1837 and 1839. Located in nearby Vacherie, Louisiana, it features tours and a bed-and-breakfast.*

Facing page: *Rocking chairs and a stone water vessel greet visitors to the porch of Laura Plantation in Vacherie, on Louisiana Highway 18.*

Above: *This Chalmette Battlefield cannon gives mute testament to the Battle of New Orleans, the 1815 confrontation that ended in Andrew Jackson's defeat of the British redcoats.*

Above: *The stunning San Francisco Plantation in Reserve, Louisiana, gets its name from* sans frusquin, *a French Creole slang phrase meaning "without a penny."*

Right: *This young antebellum-outfitted lady awaits a carriage ride at Destrehan Plantation. Destrehan is located at 13034 River Road, just fifteen minutes from New Orleans proper.*

Facing page: *This 1834 Bayou St. John plantation home now serves as the parish rectory for Our Lady of Rosary Catholic Church.*

Spectacles and Festivals of the Crescent City

The spirit of celebration in New Orleans is second to none, and throughout the year there are countless parties and events to suit any taste—just remember, it's not a real festival unless there's crawfish and a parade. Some folks shy away from Mardi Gras but love the more mellow Jazz and Heritage Festival. Others prefer the small celebrations that take place in and around the city like the Crawfish Festival or the Los Islenos Festival. Probably the best thing about these celebrations is the atmosphere that lets you observe, participate, or just relax, eat your crawfish, and watch the parade!

Mardi Gras, the city's largest spectacle, attracts more than one million revelers each year. The pre-Lenten Carnival season is intended as one last hurrah before the forty days of penance beginning on Ash Wednesday and ending with Easter. Mardi Gras starts on Twelfth Night, January 6, and culminates on Fat Tuesday with a daylong celebration of parades and costumed merriment in the streets. The city shuts down for business that day so stake your spot on St. Charles Avenue to see the Zulu parade (watch out for the decorated coconuts thrown from this krewe!); wave to the King of Carnival in the Rex parade; then head down to the French Quarter where the more risqué participants cavort in costumes and exhibitionists on balconies are eager to show you what's under theirs. Be careful, however. Carnival-goers do sometimes get arrested when they comply with "show me yours" requests.

New Orleans festivals are free and attract many generations of people from every social stratum. These celebrations are an opportunity to join a group of people who know how to have fun without taking themselves too seriously—which, come to think of it, isn't a bad way to live indeed!

Above: *A colorful float depicts the ritual of throwing beads and trinkets to the clamoring crowds below. In 1921, the Rex Krewe was the first to start throwing beaded necklaces.*

Facing page: *A Mardi Gras Indian displays the elaborate bead- and featherwork of his costume, which can take up to an entire year to create. "Indians" are comprised mostly of local African Americans who have historically identified with Native Americans.*

Facing page: *Revelers show their colors at the New Orleans Jazz and Heritage Festival. More than half a million people attend the annual event, which takes place the last weekend of April and the first weekend of May.*

Top left: *Marlon Jordan ignites the Jazz Fest. Considered the birthplace of jazz, New Orleans's musical gatherings of people of color in the 1800s at Congo Square formed the beginnings of this musical style.*

Top right: *Michael Doucet plays his fiddle with enthusiasm at the Jazz Fest. Cajun music gained worldwide attention after the 1984 Louisiana World's Fair, which showcased the state's culture.*

Left: *Grammy-winning R & B performer and New Orleans native Dr. John belts out his signature sounds at the Jazz Fest.*

Top left: *A carnival-like atmosphere prevails on the Midway of the Crawfish Festival, held every March in St. Bernard parish.*

Top right: *Buckwheat Zydeco is shown here on accordion with his band mate on the washboard-derived* frottoir, *both instruments popular in zydeco music.*

Right: *Love 'dem mud bugs! The ritual of sucking the heads of crawfish allows the seasoned juices from the boil to come through.*

Facing page: *Colorful umbrellas are essential accessories for a proper second-line parade like this one at the Jazz Fest. Derived from the jazz funeral, the second-line has evolved into an impromptu group dance at public gatherings.*

Above: *The blessing of the fleet, seen here at the Shrimp and Petroleum Festival, involves prayers and holy water offered by a priest who asks for both a bountiful season and the safety of the shrimpers. Louisiana's oldest state-chartered harvest festival was founded in 1936.*

Right: *Young members of the Spring Fiesta Queen's court in Jackson Square pose together just after the crowning of the new queen.*

Facing page: *The Los Islenos folk dancers perform at the French Quarter Festival. These descendants from the Canary Islands speak an archaic Spanish.*

Facing page: *A bird's-eye view of the French Quarter Festival showcases the Pontalba Apartments. Held every April, the French Quarter Festival usually enjoys sunny skies and ideal low-humidity temperatures in the 70s.*

Above: *A French Quarter Festival favorite, the Storyville Stompers brass band stomps out traditional sounds. "Storyville" is the name of New Orleans's former red light district where jazz great Louis Armstrong grew up.*

Left: *Cajun two-stepping is popular at Swamp Fest. Held over two weekends in October, the festivities include Cajun and zydeco musical acts and craft demonstrations throughout the Audubon Zoological Park.*

Above: *Festival queens from all of Louisiana's area festivals serve on the court of the new Floral Trails Queen.*

Facing page: *Spring Fiesta maids in antebellum dresses share an abundance of flowers with parade spectators, helping to celebrate the spring season.*

Facing page: *Merrymakers smile in front of Jackson Square. The tradition of parading in costume dates back to the 1830s, when people were seen in the street wearing costumes en route to masked balls.*

Above: *Revelers await the popular costume contest, in which they are judged for the most elaborate (usually over-the-top female impersonating) outfit. The contest is held on the corner of Bourbon and Dumaine Streets on Mardi Gras morning.*

Left: *A masked rider in the Rex Parade takes aim as he firmly clutches a necklace of beads to throw.*

Overleaf: *A float from the Krewe of Thoth parades on the Sunday before Mardi Gras (French for "Fat Tuesday"). This krewe, or organization, has been in existence since 1947.*

Index

Where to Go for More Information

New Orleans Metropolitan Convention
and Visitors Bureau
1520 Sugar Bowl Drive
New Orleans, LA 70112
504-566-5011 or 800-672-6124
www.nawlins.com

NewOrleans.com L.L.C.
3445 N. Causeway Blvd, St. 400
Metairie, LA 70002
504-309-1004
www.neworleans.com

New Orleans Tourism Marketing Corp.
One Canal Place
365 Canal Street, Suite 1120
New Orleans, LA 70130
www.neworleansonline.com

Louisiana Department of Tourism
P.O. Box 94291
Baton Rouge, LA 70804-9291
225-342-8100
www.louisianatravel.com

About the Author and Photographer

Jan Arrigo was born and raised in New Orleans and graduated from Loyola University. The former assistant editor of the local magazine *The Alligator*, she has also written numerous travel and cultural articles and has contributed to *The American Art Book*, *The Encyclopedia of Sculpture*, and *Readers Digest* magazine. Arrigo is the author of *Manhattan with a Twist: The Classic Saloons of New York City* (forthcoming) and is currently working on a book about the New Orleans food scene. She also sings as a "Ukelady" with "The Hoppin Haole Brothers," a sanctified ukulele band.

Photograph © Amelia Durand

Laura A. McElroy of Atlanta, Georgia, is a freelance photographer whose work has been published in *Diversion Travel* magazine, the *Insight Guide* on the Old South, *Western Horse*, *Travel Holiday*, and more. In addition, her New Orleans images appear on postcards, notecards, and in a regional cookbook. McElroy has had a love affair with the Big Easy since she first visited it as a teenager and says that the city's unique combination of the unexpected and the traditional makes New Orleans a photographer's paradise.

Photograph © Richard Russell